My Fur Fix

by

Lynne Bodry Shuman

Gotham Books

30 N Gould St.
Ste. 20820, Sheridan, WY 82801
https://gothambooksinc.com/

Phone: 1 (307) 464-7800

© 2024 *Lynne Bodry Shuman*. All rights reserved.

No part of this book may be reproduced, stored in a retrieval system, or transmitted by any means without the written permission of the author.

Published by Gotham Books (April 9, 2024)

ISBN: 979-8-88775-907-4 (H)
ISBN: 979-8-88775-905-0 (P)
ISBN: 979-8-88775-906-7 (E)

Because of the dynamic nature of the Internet, any web addresses or links contained in this book may have changed since publication and may no longer be valid.

The views expressed in this work are solely those of the author and do not necessarily reflect the views of the publisher, and the publisher hereby disclaims any responsibility for them.

CONTENT

DEDICATION... v

CHAPTER 1 1

CHAPTER 2 5

CHAPTER 3 7

CHAPTER 4 10

CHAPTER 5 13

CHAPTER 6 15

CHAPTER 7 18

CHAPTER 8 25

CHAPTER 9 29

CHAPTER 10 32

CHAPTER 11 48

CHAPTER 12 49

CHAPTER 13 54

CHAPTER 14 57

CHAPTER 15 62

ABOUT THE AUTHOR 76

DEDICATION

I dedicate this book to all my friends and family members who have accompanied me through the many years of joy and sadness that have been the celebration of all these beautiful pets.

Except for our entertaining Schipperkes, Schotzie and Buster, and our energetic Toodle, Murphy T. Muffin, all of our pets have been rescues. They have brought such joy and fulfillment to our lives. Every one is preciously remembered.

I hope you enjoy getting to know them, too.

And to all of you who have had your own experiences loving and caring for these special, loving, furry creatures.

CHAPTER

The day had no promise. It was a typical February morning of indiscriminate character. As I enjoyed my first wake-up sip of freshly brewed coffee, I looked through the window above the kitchen sink to randomly assess the bleakness of my postage stamp back yard.

Patches of white from a leftover snowstorm added a bit of interest to an otherwise colorless garden. Even the evergreens were listless.

Then, out of the corner of my left eye, there was a flash of gold as two, tiny, longhaired kittens romped and wrestled along the fence, darting in and out between the sleeping peony bushes.

As my eyes focused better, their mother came into view. She was also longhaired, about the shade of weathered grey stone. Much the matron, she was sitting very patiently as the golden fur balls used her for their bank shots into the lavender. Joining them was a third longhaired acrobat – this one the color of the mother, but with a distinctive gold emblem on its face.

I guess I must have moved – I don't remember doing so – but something caught the mother's attention. She cast a look of alarm at my window and hastened along the railroad tie that separated the flower beds, calling for the 3 bouncing babies to follow.

It was then-- and only then—that I saw she had a fourth kitten. It was a shorthair, the very same color as Mom, and had been cuddled between her front legs as she sat as sentinel. She and this kitten were as one until it spilled out into the phlox bed as she hastened away to safety.

It was February. It was cold. What was a mother cat doing outside in this freezing weather with 4 kittens about 5 weeks old? Were they out for a morning romp? Or had they been born under a porch somewhere in the middle of winter and only knew the cold?   I obsessed on this all day.

What could I do to provide shelter for this feral family? I took mental inventory of the materials at hand in the basement and the garage. I even called my daughter in Cleveland for suggestions, since she had already been through this situation at her house -- not being at liberty to bring in new animals because of established household pets. For me, it was a 10 year old male rescue cat who owned my home.

For 2 days I mentally planned and prepared—all to no avail, since they never came back.

Then, one morning in the heat of July, as if by magic, there they were again—a bit larger now, but just as playful. This time they stayed. This time the weather was agreeable, so staying under the deck where the ground was cool was welcoming. This time I went to the feed store and bought a 1-ton bag of kitten chow. I meant to nourish them for a longggg time.

And so began a love affair.

Every morning, I took dry food and water to the center of the deck-- placing it where the kittens could easily find it and I could easily observe them through the kitchen window over the sink.

Cautiously, the mother approached the food – being ever mindful of any detectable movement through the window.... After all, there was a monster beyond, you know.

Curiously, the kittens sampled this new, crunchy stuff that mom said was O.K. to eat.

I chose kitten food reasoning that the mother would also benefit – or at least would not be harmed – by the nutrition meant for the young-ones.

Each morning, I took them food and water. Each afternoon, after their naps on the wicker porch chairs, I watched them cavort among the daylilies and garden statues.

The two golden cherubs were virtual twins. The only discernible difference being that one had a broad white blaze down the center of his nose.

The two grey kittens were easier to identify... one had long hair with a splash of gold on its face, the other was a short hair with absolutely no memorable markings. In fact, it was on the homely side.

At this time, there was no way to ascertain their gender, but I named them anyway, according to their personalities.

The golden twins were Jackie and Zack – rather interchangeably at this point. The longhaired grey was Lucy and the short haired grey, Amanda.

Mama Cat remained Mama Cat. I tried to name her Sarah, but it just didn't stick. She was much more than a simple appellation.

By the end of July, Lucy had disappeared. Since we live in a small city where neighborhood back yards abut, my heart and mind would only accept that someone else found her as adorable as I had and took her inside to love and to cherish.

Then there were three.

CHAPTER

From time to time, other adult cats – male, would be my guess – appeared to share a dinner on the deck: A large yellow shorthair, a scruffy grey longhair, and a noble black shorthair with intelligent eyes. They would eat, lounge around for a while, maybe play with the kittens a bit, but ultimately disappear.

By August, Mama Cat was absent, sometime for days, but the kittens stayed.

Late one afternoon, my next door neighbors were in their backyard and their normally closed gate was uncharacteristically open. I took advantage of the anomaly and went over to say "Hi" and see if they were aware of the feral family.

Wife Judy said they were and asked me if I was feeding the kittens.

"Oh, yes!" I said. "I can't not feed them."

"Well," she said, "We've been feeding them, too.... At night."

I was delighted! I was beginning to feel responsible for their well-being—even long term—and that was becoming a bit of an issue for me. I knew I could not bring them into the house because my 10 year-old male cat MIFFIN was already growling at them through the window.

The interior of the house was his personal domain not to be shared with these upstarts. (Actually, he isn't all that happy about other humans coming to visit, either.)

Judy went on to tell me how much they enjoyed the kittens. Her husband was a twin and they had twin grandchildren. They felt the golden siblings were twins also and felt a familial connection to them.

Alas, however, they too could not take them inside their house, but they surely enjoyed them outside. She and her husband spent every summer evening on the patio enjoying an after dinner cocktail and watching the circus troupe.

In their yard, they had children's toys for their twin grandchildren including a plastic slide about 4 feet high and a tree house with a ladder-like stairway about 7 feet off the ground. The kittens enjoyed both. I suggested she should take a video of the adventurous scamps climbing the steps and careening down the plastic slide…. That would be a YouTube treat! She smiled and admitted they were technologically challenged and didn't know about such things.

Even still, it remained that I felt relieved that the kittens were being co-parented.

We agreed that I would feed them in the morning, and they would feed them in the evening. I would also provide water to eliminate the daily search for such.

CHAPTER

Mama Cat appeared now and then. She seemed healthy, as in "not skinny". On one visit, Jackie came up the steps from the garden to say "hi" while she was eating. (Jackie is like that.) Mama Cat hissed at him. I could just read his thoughts as he stopped short and sat on the second step, watching her.

"But, Mom, it's me, Jackie. Gee, it's good to see you, again. How have you been?" But Mama Cat ignored him and, when finished eating, left the yard by way of the driveway—completely avoiding the backyard where her three offspring were playing.

My backyard is small – maybe 25 feet square. Along the left fence is a 3 foot wide flower bed edged with railroad ties. In this area grow the Peony bushes, the day lilies, and some lavender. Along the back fence are hostas, one stately Yucca, and a healthy Rhododendron in the corner. To the right is the garage, lined with more lilies, and one stoic climbing rose.

Long ago, I replaced the grass in the center with a patio. I had no time to mow this 15 foot square patch of ragged green lawn... it was either change to pavers, or buy a goat.

The patio is a diamond shape with the corners at North, South, East and West. West is toward the left fence, east is toward the garage, south is toward the house and deck and kitchen window. Each corner is a flower bed and space for garden sculptures.

Over time, simple, meaningful pieces have come to live in my garden. One piece is a two foot tall, green, metal frog playing a yellow violin. His name is Mr. Hippensteel... a memento from a delightful mountain vacation. Another is a bit larger – a cement bench on which sit a boy and his dog – Petey and Pup. There is also a small pixie named Petula who lives among the lilies. In the center of the patio is a round, iron, ice cream table and four chairs with cushions.... the location of many an afternoon nap.

I bring this information about the backyard to the story to describe the environment within which the kittens spent their day.

Several times a day I looked out the kitchen window and enjoyed the activity. On occasion I have been able to capture this circus with my camera – that is, **if** it is close-by, and **if** I can get it zoomed and focused after taking what seems forever to turn on.... And **if** the scenario I had hope to preserve is still the same – or at least similar to the reason for reaching for the camera in the first place.

CHAPTER

The summer progressed. The kittens grew. The feline visitors came and went, but the kittens stayed – romping during the day in my yard and entertaining in the evenings in the neighbor's yard where they enjoyed supper and comfortable sleeping arrangements. But, they were back to my yard each morning for the breakfast buffet.

Fall arrived and with it came Mama Cat with two new kittens – 1 yellow, 1 grey – both long hair. Both about 5 weeks old. It was a bit like watching a rerun.

The little ones romped and tumbled while Mama Cat stayed, watchfully, close by. A favorite activity was chasing Mama's tail. Mama spent a leisurely moment of rest on the sun-warmed driveway, obligingly twitching her long, furry, grey tail for the little ones to pounce upon and tumble after.

Being that small, again, there was no way to detect their gender, but, based on their personalities, I have named them, none-the-less. The yellow ball of fluff is Katie Kat and the grey fur ball is Freddie. He just looks like a Freddie.

Now there were five.

Although Mama Cat brought Katie and Freddie every morning, they didn't get the human contact that the first litter had been exposed to.

When I started feeding the first family of kittens, I was silent as I placed the food in their dinner plate dish and the water in their small, pyrex flat baking dish—(flat so it wouldn't get tipped over) .... They got used to my presence and the food. Then, after a week or so, each morning as I took food out on the deck, I talked to them. They were wary at first, peeking at me from behind the wicker, and didn't approach the food until I was back in the house. After a week or two, they gathered around the food while I was still there and still talking. Another week or so and I was able to carefully touch each one. They didn't accept it at first, but soon trusted that I was safe. In time, I was able to pick each one up – only briefly, but they became used to being handled. It had been a very long process.

In the evening, they romped at the neighbor's and even climbed up on the laps in lounge chairs to accept a petting.

But, now it was fall. The protective awning over the deck had been put away, exposing the dry food to the elements, and the furniture had been stored in the garage. It became obvious that the breakfast bar had to be moved inside the garage as well.

All three older kittens, Jackie, Zack and grey Amanda, adapted to the new location, readily. The door was left propped open so they could come and go freely. But, the opportunity to socialize the new kittens was not there. Mama Cat kept them separate. They only came to eat after I had disappeared into the house.

CHAPTER

Now, Cold weather was coming. The leaves of summer had turned and fallen. The garden was no longer vibrant. My conscience would not rest until I could provide a warm, comfortable place for them in the garage. I knew they had some areas at the neighbors, but they sounded rather random.... a cushion in a treehouse, a hole under a shed. It took some detective work, but I came up with an assortment of materials with which I could create some comfortable and, hopefully warm, areas --- either for one or for all. There was a large plastic table top that could be put in place for a wind break. There was a carpet remnant that would fit across the length of the settee to keep their paws dry and warm above the cold, damp, cement garage floor. But the most creative cubby came with a collection of unlikely components.

In the back of the garage was a double dresser with deep drawers. It was there when I bought the property. If I were a better gardener, the drawers would probably be full of gardening supplies, but since that is not the case, they were empty.... all 8 of them. Hmmmmm.

If I staggered opening them, they would offer individual nests for the kittens and/or Mom and the new babies.

Nearby were wire forms used to support growing tomato plants. — an intended project one summer until I discovered really great tasting tomatoes were already available at the local farm market for much less financial investment and stress than growing my own. These wire structures had potential.

Taking strong vise grips, I bent the bottom legs of the wire cages sideways to form a flat bottom basket. Over the frame, I placed an old pillow case, then a plastic kitchen trash bag to create a weather barrier, then an old sweatshirt for some warmth. Finally, inside, I placed an old pillow for comfort. Three of these were fashioned and then each was placed in an open drawer. They just fit. They could work. My conscience was appeased.

The next morning, as I picked up each kitten, I put them into one of the nests. They didn't stay, of course, it was breakfast time, and they had better things to do, but they knew of their existence.

From time to time, I would check the nests and find dirty paw prints on the pillowcases, so someone was going in there at some time. Without a surveillance camera, it would not be known who.... But that seemed a bit excessive.

 It felt good that the project had been successful.

CHAPTER

Amanda was the most wary of the three remaining adolescents. Her favorite napping spot was behind the wicker love seat, not up on the seat. She was always the last to come to breakfast... bolting at the slightest noise or movement. It took her the longest to become comfortable hearing my voice, or feeling my gentle touch while she ate. Amanda was probably 9 months old before she would let me pick her up briefly... and then, only after she had seen the twins successfully returned to the ground having survived the dreaded morning cuddling. But, after a while, she seemed to look forward to this morning ritual. She began to trust enough that she wouldn't begin to eat until after she had been picked up for her morning cuddles.

Having been the ugly duckling as a kitten, she had grown into a lovely adolescent with a sweet personality and a powerful purr.

Amanda, or Mandy, as she became more socialized, didn't always hang with the others...... Often, in the morning, she was the last to arrive.... coming up the driveway from the front of the house – whereas, the twins came across the backyards from the neighbors. ... coming only after she heard me calling for her to come have breakfast.

Mama Cat, Katie and Freddie seemed to come from the adjacent garage.... although Katie often went under the house next door where a brick was missing from the foundation of a small rear addition.

Christmas was quickly approaching. My grown children and grandchildren would soon be arriving for the holidays. They would finally meet these creatures that had dominated my phone conversations for most of the year.

My daughter came first. On her first morning here, she came with me to feed the kittens. As I picked up one, I would hand it to her for cuddles. Amanda was the first, then Jackie, then Zack.

That was the last time we saw Amanda. She didn't appear the next day – Christmas Day. Every part of my soul believes that someone took her in as a Christmas present and she now has a warm and loving home.

And then there were four.

CHAPTER

Winter is here in a BIG way!

The golden twins had developed good thick undercoats. I could feel it when I picked them up each morning. From the looks of the little ones, Katie and Freddie, they had good winter coats as well. Mama Cat had already survived at least one bitter winter, so I was sure she knew how and where to stay warm. But the forecast was for about a week of sub-zero temperatures augmented with strong wind chills in the vicinity of –12 to –20 degrees. I wasn't as convinced any of the kittens would share her experience or knowledge—or would stay with her in her secret havens.

Although there were several padded, protective cubbies set up in the garage, my conscience wouldn't rest until I attempted to create a better environment. I set up soft areas in the basement, prepared litter boxes and feeding stations, and unlocked the grade door to the driveway. Rationalization told me the members of the feral family I could catch would be safe there for a few days until the frigid weather moved on.

Catching them was the operative word. Although Mama Cat had reached the point of staying calm at my presence, she always kept a safe distance away -- ready to escape if I attempted to move in her direction. She was a wary one.

Freddie and Katie Kat had absolutely no idea who or what I was, except that when I was no longer within sight, food had appeared. I was sure they thought of me as some huge, scary monster to avoid at any cost. My hopes of gathering any of them were almost zero.

The twins, however, were already poised at the back door that morning to accompany the food-lady to the garage for hugs and breakfast buffet. Instead, I scooped them up and took them to the basement. It wasn't a great distance from the garage to the grade door, but with all their wiggling, I was afraid that one would jump out of my arms before I could get them into the house. It seemed to take forever, but actually, It all happened so quickly they weren't sure what the situation was, except the indoor surroundings were new and the air was warmer. Although the house is kept at 68 degrees, the basement was probably closer to 58.

I showed them the food, water, beds, and litter box – now that was new and strange – not sure what that is for....

They seemed fine, eager to explore these new surroundings, so I came upstairs and shut the door to continue on with a long day's list of errands and appointments.

About 4 PM – I stopped at the neighbors to let them know where the twins were, and that this internment was only temporary, until the weather became a comfortable degree above zero. Since they fed them in the evening, I knew they would wonder where they were.

Then, after setting down my assorted belongings, and hanging up my winter coat, I went to the basement to say "hi" to the kittens, to check on their food, and to spend some time playing with them. I expected to be greeted at the foot of the stairs by eager, hungry kittens, but no one appeared. I called, but heard no response. Now, there are lots of places in a basement to hide, and Zack – by now determined to be the male -- had seemed a little anxious, but Jackie

– with all the characteristics of being female -- had seemed totally fine.

I walked the perimeter of the basement talking to them all the while. Then, finally, I heard a faint meow from the far corner.... there were fairly large storage boxes over there. Perhaps they had gotten into a tall box and couldn't get out. But that was not the case. Even though I was close to the wall, the mews still sounded far away. ... I moved boxes and old doors leaning against the wall.... nothing... I went upstairs to get a powerful flashlight and returned to the far corner.

Shining the strong beam of light around the floors and corners, I found nothing, but still heard the faint mewing. I switched the beam to the ceiling and my heart sank to the pit of my stomach.

Now, my house was built in 1914, but in the late '70s the owners took on a renovation. They converted the porch, which ran the entire length of the back of the house, into a kitchen and powder room. The kitchen followed the original foundation footprint, but the powder room needed new foundations and outer walls... creating its own, separate, inaccessible basement room about 5 feet square and 7 feet deep.

In the header, at the top of the wall, was a hole about 5 inches high and 8 inches long – just the right size for curious kittens to fit through. The tall boxes and new soil pipe were great stepping stones to reach that hole. And you know how curious kittens can be.

Could they be in that sealed off space? Were they on the floor of it... too deep to reach the hole to get back out? My heart was pounding furiously in my chest, my mind was spinning with ideas that might work to extricate them.   It was past 5:00 now.... Who could be reached if I needed help?

When I bought this house, 17 years ago, my children had bought me a cordless drill. It was handy right there on the basement work bench. Could I drill through the mortar and make a hole in the brick foundation wall? Would the drill have enough power? ..... Not with dead batteries, it won't. I plugged in the charger and set one of the batteries in place. From my dad I inherited an old, metal Band-Aid box full of assorted drill bits......The Band Aid box miraculously contained a masonry bit, but it wasn't long enough to reach all the way through the thickness of the bricks..... and where would be the best place to drill to not collapse the house?

Against one wall was propped a free-standing storage closet.... wide, but not too tall.... and not too deep. I had never put anything in it, so it wasn't very heavy, only awkward. I moved it away from the wall, hoping to find a miracle. Behind it, the wall looked as if a section had been replaced.... Perhaps this was the opening for the workmen to enter the space to install the heating duct and plumbing. The mortar was different and the workmanship was not quite the same quality. Above it all, was a full-length steel I-beam supporting the house, so this short wall was not critical.

I would start here. I would take out enough bricks to create an opening big enough for cats to fit through and find freedom. But, it would have to wait until tomorrow when I could buy a longer drill bit and both batteries would be fully charged.

Not entirely satisfied, but feeling there were some viable answers, I reassured the kittens I would get them out and went upstairs.

I needed to call my daughter, she always has sensible ideas and should be home from work by now. With the first words, she immediately detected the fear and anxiety in my voice. I tried to explain the situation calmly, accurately, constructively while thinking, "For all my well-meaning plans to prolong their lives, I have lost the kittens forever!" It is a very sharp and hollow edge between hope and terror.

My daughter listened patiently and finally said, in a very calm voice, "Mother, you have not lost the kittens. You can get them out."

I felt she was saying this to calm my mind and get me to focus.

She continued, "do you have a long piece of cloth and a long strong stick?"

Immediately, I grasped the concept of this ingenious idea. "Yes!" I said, "I have a sheet in the linen closet. I will tie one corner to a stick or broom handle. I am sure there is something in this house that will work!"

I couldn't hang up the phone fast enough. I grabbed an old pink sheet from the upstairs linen closet – not even sure what size it was... it didn't matter! It was going to save the kittens!

On the way down the basement stairs I saw an old plunger.... Perfect! I tied one corner of the sheet firmly to the plunger handle and lowered the other into the abyss.... braced the plunger handle across the hole to bear any weight.... and talked to the kittens.

Would this be enough to entice them to come out? Food! Food will coax them to climb the Rapunzel – style ladder to safety. It was back upstairs to search the cupboard where Miffin's food was stored. Then, back to the basement with stronger feelings of hope. I made a grand and noisy practice of snapping open the can and spooning it into a soup bowl.... waving it ceremoniously across the opening, hoping the draft of cold air would take it to the kittens. Then, I placed the aromatic food on the floor in a large open space, where they could be comfortable eating... and leaving the lights on for them to see, whatever time of night they chose to be brave, ... came back upstairs to wait for sure success...... With all my being, I hoped!

Feeling better about the situation, I called my daughter back to let her know that her brilliant suggestion had worked. She further suggested that I find a long board to lower into the hole creating a ramp. Wrapping it with cloth would offer texture for grip.

Not as confident I would find this last item, I set off on the quest. I did find a long piece of molding in the basement rafters, but a heating duct prohibited a workable angle for this additional step. I did not consider this a set-back. The original idea seemed plausible enough.

Again, I heard the mewing. This time it seemed louder.... closer.... And then, there she was – Jackie had appeared from nowhere and was doing figure eights around my ankles.

There are no words to express my relief! I scooped her up, took her upstairs and closed the door to prevent her from returning to the basement. My mind reeled with a token feeling of peace! One was safe! One more to go!

I still don't know where she had come from.... But, it was time to let go of the "What ifs", move forward with her safety and comfort, and trust that Zack would follow.

Upstairs, I prepared a new feeding area in the kitchen and litter box in the notorious powder room. She seemed content, but I held her the entire evening, even staying up to watch every last minute of a late TV show I would ordinarily have recorded to watch another time. I didn't mind.

But, it was approaching midnight and I needed to go to bed. Making sure Miffin was not in the back section of the house, I closed it up, leaving Jackie there and went upstairs. She would be comfortable in a confined space. She had food, water, a litter box, and the family room furniture to sleep on or hide beneath.

Miffin had his food, water and litter box accessible to him in the upstairs bathroom, but, I knew he was still displeased with me.... he didn't sleep in his usual place on my bed that night.

CHAPTER

The next morning, opening the kitchen door, I expected to be greeted by a happy Jackie. But, again, she was nowhere to be found. This time there was no panic. I knew, in spite of all her long, thick, fluffy fur, she was structurally a tiny lady. She could hide in the smallest area.

But, as I talked to her and made food prep noises, she was suddenly, quietly at my ankles, purring loudly. I picked her up for morning cuddles. She ate breakfast, used the litter box, and was content to stay with me.

After being sure she and Miffin were both ready for the day, I ignored my anxieties and headed for the basement. Still, no sign of Zack. The flavorful, canned food had not been touched. I checked the sheet to be sure it was still secure and went back upstairs, but this time, I left the basement door open..... hoping against hope that Jackie would stay with me and not go downstairs, again.

In fact, feeling quite at home, she followed me to the second floor where I would stay busy and she could explore new areas.

It was mid-morning. I was working at the computer in my second floor office. Jackie was in and out of this room and the bedrooms . MIffin was somewhere, sulking.

From somewhere in the house I heard a crash. Hmmm. Had Jackie jumped up on a table and knocked over a lamp? Pushed a Candy dish to the floor? A knick-knack?

I went to investigate. Nothing on the second floor. Maybe the first floor. On the way down the stairs I heard a meow. I thought it was Jackie.... Perhaps frightened by the sound of the crash.... The meow was coming from the living room.

At the front window of the living room, between two easy chairs, there is a drum table covered with a floor-length cloth. Next to the wall, under the cloth, is an air vent which keeps the area under the table warm in the winter and cool in the summer. It is Miffin's favorite place to hide.... A logical first place to check.

Lifting the table skirt I saw a yellow cat, but it was not Miffin....the hair was too long. Maybe it was Jackie, but, when I could see the face.... The face with the white blaze on the nose, my knees went weak....IT WAS ZACK!

I sat on the floor to talk with him. He was beyond my reach. Coaxing him to me seemed logical. But, it wasn't working. I brought his food to the Living Room. Nope. Not interested. After about 5 minutes, a curious Jackie appeared. She went right up to him and nuzzled his face. He seemed to relax.

Grasping the opportunity, while Jackie licked his ears and reassured Zack that all was safe, I ran to close the basement door..... let's make a change in this equation! Let's remove the entire category of basement and all its horrors!

O.K. Now, It is time to take a minute......time to take a few deep breaths.... Time to be extremely thankful. Both kittens are now safe and well inside the house.... something I said I would never do.   So far, it isn't terrible.

While Zack gets comfortable and Jackie assures him all is safe, I head for the basement to reclaim the sheet and plug up EVERY hole in every header with custom cut foam pieces left from a former project. BONUS Sub zero air is no longer streaming into my house. After 17 years, how did I NOT know about these holes?

Satisfied that all danger in the basement had been erased, I returned to the main floor and securely closed the dreaded basement door. It was now past noon. Once, again, all seemed right with the world. And I realized that I was hungry.

While preparing my lunch, I found the source of the crash sound.... Apparently, when Zack came up from the basement, he went to explore this new territory and headed for the kitchen where he jumped up on the sink to look out the same kitchen window from which I first observed them, so many months earlier. On the windowsill there had been a pair of handblown glass birds from a long ago visit to Venice, Italy. Those birds were now in the stainless-steel sink.... Either having been pushed from the sill or jumped in self-defense upon seeing this golden ogre. Regardless of how they got there, they had made a substantial noise. The noise must have frightened Zack sending him to the opposite end of the house and under the living room table.

By the end of the day, Zack had explored the first floor and was feeling comfortable. Jackie was happy to sit on my lap, and Miffin was letting everyone know of his disapproval, making routine strolls through the family room -- practicing his hissing and growling. He was very vocal, but not physically aggressive. (Like an old curmudger yelling at the kids to get off his lawn.) Jackie and Zack, now curled up together next to me on the couch, watched him curiously, wondering, "Why are you doing that? Do you have a problem?"

I am thankful for our progress.

CHAPTER

For 4 days and nights the temperature was subzero. For 4 days and nights the twins stayed inside. During the day, they stayed hidden somewhere in the house, but about supper time they would appear for food and socializing. I closed off the kitchen and family room to keep them in a smaller space, and when I went to bed, they stayed overnight in this area. Miffin did decide to come back to spend his nights in his usual spot up on my bed on the second floor. By now, he was content to stay separate and grudgingly let those intruders have the run of the first floor.

During these four days, I watched the weather forecasts to see if this frigid wave would ever cease. I also kept taking food out to the garage hoping Mama Cat and Katie and Freddie were surviving on their own. I had looked into trying to catch them in a Hava Heart trap and taking them to the local animal shelter, but was told that if they were not socialized, they would be euthanized.... The shelter already had too many other strays to care for. Since these were not technically strays, but feral, I feared for their well-being and hoped they would find refuge together and would survive the cold on their own.

One afternoon, I did see Mama Cat resting on the driveway, and another day, I saw Katie Kat darting into the garage. Each day the food was gone, so hopefully, they were getting the nourishment and not the neighborhood squirrels. I also hoped that they were finding warmth and shelter among the nests that had been created for them in the dresser drawers.

Well, the day has finally arrived. Temperatures will reach 40 degrees during the day today and roughly 17 degrees overnight, but still remain above zero. This morning, after cuddles and breakfast, I opened the back door to let them leave the house on their own terms.

Zack went first. Jackie took a little longer, but once out, she went straight for the garage. Zack turned, sat down on the driveway and looked questioningly at the closed door. He seemed to be thinking, "How come?" "Why are we out here? Was it something we said?"

About that time Katie Kat came bounding out from under the car, which was parked in the driveway, to greet the twins and they all disappeared into the garage.

I haven't seen Freddie yet, but winter is far from over. When spring arrives will there be still more fluffy, scampering kittens? Or will the final words of this story be

"And then there were two."

I will keep watch.... on them and on the weather forecast. And I will continue to take breakfast and water out each morning.... We will see if this was a one-time adventure, or will become a normal way to get through winter on the banks of the Ohio River.

CHAPTER

A page has turned. A new chapter has opened.... Jackie has returned to the outside world.

Yesterday, I obsessed about when and whether she should go outside again. She and Miffin were becoming friends. She is SO easy as an inside cat.... So loveable, so accommodating, so clean..... and there is her vulnerability...

About her vulnerability... Just when the world seemed manageable, and all was going well, a crisis intruded on our idyllic life of kittenhood. It happened suddenly and mysteriously. I was setting the breakfast buffet for all the furry family, when I noticed that Jackie was acting very strangely. She wasn't tracking well. She seemed bothered by something at her right side. When I picked her up for her morning cuddle, I was greatly.... I mean, OMG WHAT HAS HAPPENED.... disturbed. Her right eye was swollen, matted, and oozing pus.

No breakfast for this lass. I immediately scooped her up and took her into the house to see if I could find a remedy. After a day or two of only somewhat successful home care, it was into the cat carrier and off to visit the vet. Examination disclosed that the eye was destroyed and had to be removed. My heart sank. The surgery would have to be done. There was such a hospital in a nearby city, so that was attainable. But, what about the expense?

There were no second thoughts. The arrangements were made and I knew the funds would come from somewhere.

I had been sharing the photos and stories of the feral family on facebook for quite awhile. The twins nearly had a page of their own.... They certainly had a following. So, I shared the story of Jackey's plight and the response was amazing! Folks sent donations from $5.00 to $100 to cover her surgery and recovery. She became the local humanitarian cause. She even was lovingly dubbed our "One Eyed Jack'.

I would like to share those facebook messages with you, now.

Feb 15.

Update on the feral family..... Jackie is in the house with me. When I went to feed our furry family Wednesday morning, she came stumbling into the garage. When I picked her up it turns out she couldn't see out of one eye. It was mattered shut. With warm water and cotton balls we have gotten it cleaned up, but I fear there is a deeper problem. I think she is on her way to her first visit to the vet. Hope it is nothing serious. She is so sweet.

I brought Jackie into the house and bathed her eye with warm water and cotton balls. In time, the first layer of crust came off. That was Wednesday. By Friday, it was looking better, but not well. She was eating and drinking water and sleeping on my lap (and not under the chair).

A call to the animal shelter and a visit to the pharmacist gave me more information about what I might be dealing with. A festered eye can be the result of a scratch, an allergy, a virus. I picked up eye drops to treat an allergy, just in case. With all the feral and visiting cats, it could be the result of a scratch from an altercation trying to protect the mother from the visitors. If it was a virus, it would be contagious, so it was good that I took her inside away from the rest of the feral family.

Over the weekend the eye seemed to rally with less reddening and less swelling, but was not any better overall.

This morning (Monday), I made an appointment for her very first visit to the vet. The good news is that Jackie/Jacky (It turns out she is really a he) is in overall good health.

The sad news is that the eye is gone. Jacky will lose his right eye. It is either operate to remove the eye or put him down. When I heard the news, I had to sit down and not be sick to my stomach. Several deep breaths and a drink of cold water and I was prepared for the whole diagnosis. After agonizing assessment, my decision was to save this loveable cat and have the eye removed.

He will be operated on late today or early tomorrow morning. While he is anesthetized, he will also be neutered. The overall cost is just over $400. (About $154 of that for the neutering.)

I felt it only fair to discuss this with the neighbors who want to keep the cats for their summer enjoyment, but are not excited about having them in the house during the winter. They have a backyard shed under which the feral family sometimes takes refuge. I was hoping they would contribute to saving one of their "twins." The immediate response was that this was not a good time for them financially. Well, it isn't a good time for anyone, right now, and this beautiful cat didn't pick the time.

I am sharing this with you, hoping that you might be able, in some small way, to help me absorb the cost of saving Jacky. I will keep him with me in the house until he is completely healed and able to, once again, join his feral family. Miffin will just have to adjust to company.

One friend has offered her "Havaheart" trap to the cause, hoping we will be able to catch the females in the family and get them neutered. The mother has beautiful kittens, but I cannot afford to be responsible, either financially or emotionally, for her wantonness.... especially if it means injuring the sons who come to her defense with visiting suitors.

If you are able to contribute, please contact me by e-mail or facebook message and I will let you know how we can make this all work.... as well as keep you informed of Jacky's condition.

I appreciate any monetary help that you can contribute.

Thank you in advance, during his recovery, and after it is all over... you have saved a life...

Feb 18

Update... Jacky is home. He is doing well wearing a stylish blue and hot pink collar. He has stitches at both ends. Right now he is trying diligently to wash, but the collar is in the way. He seems right at home. I do have pain meds, if he needs them.... of course that increased the final bill to $425.55.... but we will reach that goal, I feel positive.

Again, thank you to everyone who helped.

The surgery went well. When he came home, he was wearing a large cone collar to keep him from reaching for his eye. Eating was a challenge, but he seemed to conquer that. He lived inside the house for the duration of his recovery and acclimated very well. We became used to cuddle time.

Quite coincidentally, while he was at the vet's, we learned that under all that long, soft, glorious fur "she" was a 'he". My daughter called him an Omega male.... Whereby Zack was definitely the Alpha male in that family.

That would explain all the feminine behaviors we had been observing.... The extra affection when playing with Zack. The waiting for the younger ones to gather around the buffet. The willingness to cuddle in the evenings when Zack would rather be left alone.

Thank you to everyone! We are chipping away at the huge amount. But he is worth every penny. I saw Zack, Mom and Freddie this morning when I took out fresh water (everything is frozen) and food. The only one I haven't seen is Katie Kat.... for several days. Hoping someone has taken her inside.

Update. I checked with our shelter about vouchers and ASPCA affiliations... There are no vouchers in this area. The ASPCA seems fuzzy. I do want to thank all the caring folks who have responded for Jacky

Again, thank you, all. We are making a good dent in the costs.

Jackie is home. He is doing well wearing a stylish blue and hot pink collar to keep him away from the stitches at both ends. Right now he is trying diligently to wash, but the collar is in the way. Hmmm.... An issue... He seems right at home. I do have pain meds, if he needs them.... of course that increased the final bill to $425.55.... but we will reach that goal, I feel positive.

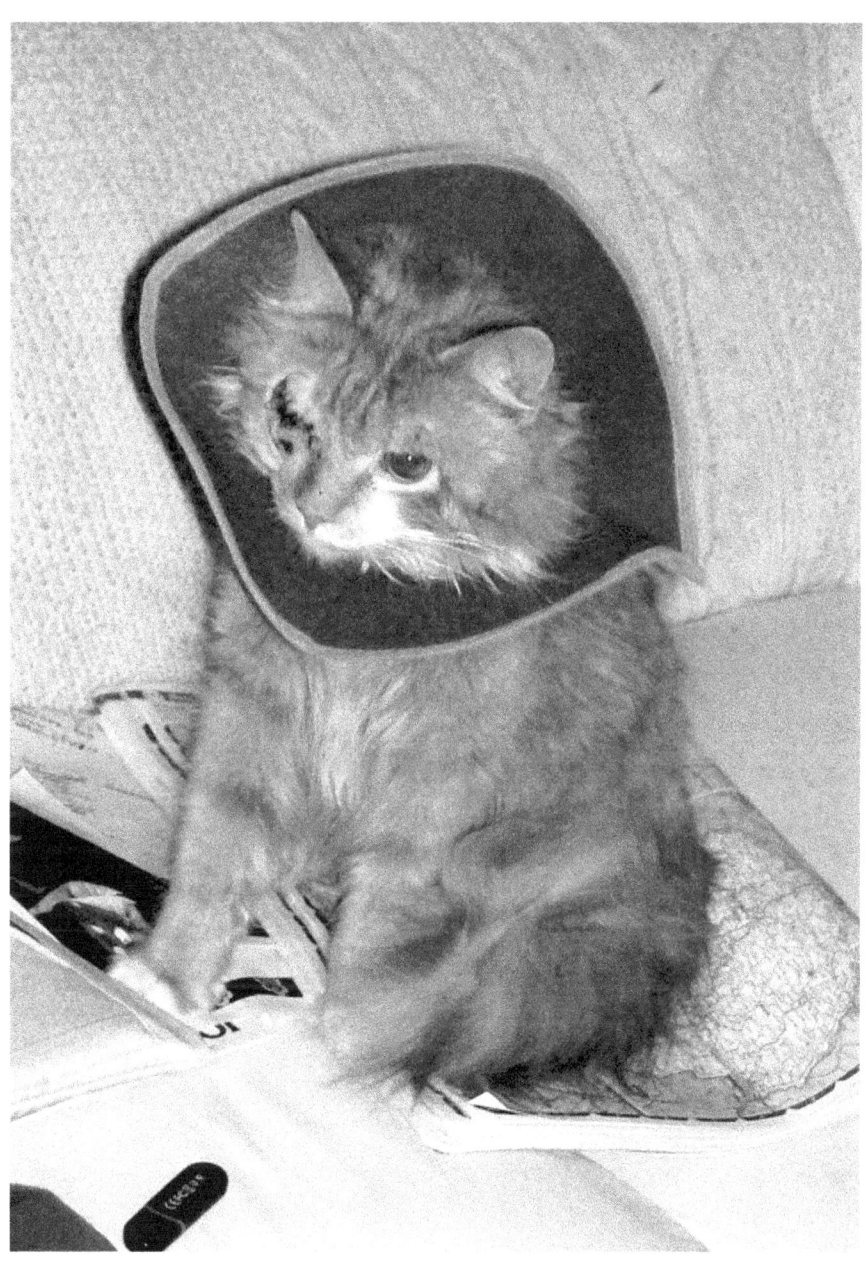

He is such a soldier. I give him his meds at night so he will sleep well. He seems to not need it during the day. Had a good breakfast this morning. The collar does get in the way, though.

I do believe Jacky is feeling better.... today he wanted to play! The eye is looking very good. The swelling has gone down and the pink is disappearing. He still sleeps most of the day, and thinks this cuddling business is a good habit.

Miffin is warming slightly. Doesn't hiss quite as loud or as long.

Feb 25, 2015

Good Morning. Jacky is adventurous this morning. After yesterday's trip to the vet and an antibiotic shot for a slight fever, he is up and running today. The swelling is much better, redness all but gone.

Forgot to have him weighed. but I no longer feel his ribs when I pick him up. I bet he's up a pound.

He went exploring upstairs, but when he was ready to come down, the Miffin monster was guarding the stairway. His solution.... just sit down until help comes.

No challenge, just acceptance of the situation...... That's Jacky. So sweet.

The vet wants to wait another week to take out the eye stitches. Maybe by then they will be BFFs. He is now having a practice nap right here next to me. Guess I will watch the news one more time.

I'm going to miss having these characters in the house. Monday will be a week. Zack seems fine. He is even letting me address some of his winter fur clumps. Jacky is an imp. He teases Zack.... and Miffin.... They take it only so long. His eye looks better than ever. Perhaps there had been some infection since the surgery.... the socket now looks like he has another eye.... not so pirate patchy. It has been rainy all week, so I am glad to know they are inside and dry.

Haven't seen the others outside. Hope they are staying warm and dry.

March 3

The gray cat is Freddie Kat.... he is from the fall litter and never became socialized. He comes each morning to eat...... after he is sure I am in the house again.... it is rare that he lingers, or sits still long enough to be photographed. They had the same mother.... not sure about the father.... mother never said. He has the same personality as the twins and Amanda (first litter). Just very skittish.

March 5

Zack this morning. Jacky is still in the house. Mucho snow last night.

March 7

Jacky is quite the curious cat...... The stitches came out on Monday. .... the collar came off on Friday...... now he is exploring the house without hindrance......that is except for Miffin. Jacky turns out to be quite a tease when it comes to Miffin. He Jumps off the wingback chair just after Miffin passes...... then RUNS the other way. Miffin is so confused......

March 9

All is well with the trump card........ one-eyed-Jack......He is adjusting quite well without his collar. Miffin is mellowing as well.

Here he is taking a lap nap.

March 15

A page has turned. A new chapter has opened.... Jacky has returned to the outside world.

Yesterday, I obsessed about when and whether he should go outside again. He and Miffin were becoming friends. He is SO easy as an inside cat.... So loveable, so accommodating, so clean..... and there is his vulnerability...

This morning, when I came in from feeding Zack and company, Jacky went outside. Without hesitation, he walked straight for the garage..... nothing wrong with his peripheral vision..... to get the messages left on the doors and boxes by the other visitors.

I watched him closely, from inside the kitchen door, as he rubbed Zack's face in greeting and explored the old stomping grounds. Then, I called the neighbor to let her know he was back outside. She said she would watch for him.

It is a bitter sweet moment. I am so glad that he is doing so well, but I will miss him in the house. He will be back visiting when Zack goes to be neutered and has to be inside for a few days while he heals. I do think having Jacky inside with him will be calming.

Miffin didn't miss a moment of Jacky's exit. As soon as I sat down with a second cup of coffee, he was on my lap...... for the first time in about a month. I'm just guessing now, but he may not miss Jacky as much as I will.

March 18

Just when I was concerned about Jacky's depth perception and peripheral vision, yesterday I found him up in the rafters of the garage...... just enjoying the view. Who knew?

March 19

This morning Jacky and Freddie were cavorting on the deck. He never missed. Guess he is pretty much back to normal. My blood pressure can now settle down.

Also saw Mom this morning when she came for breakfast. The only one missing is Katie Kat. Hope she has been taken in to a good home.

March 29

Well, the day is almost here. Tomorrow morning at 0 dark hundred, Zack goes to be neutered. I haven't told him yet.... he and Jacky came back into the house yesterday morning. (That sounds like they just willingly walked into the house.... not so, but it was easy to scoop them up and carry them in. They think it is an outing by now .... or an in-ing. I will keep Jacky inside with him as a calming influence. When the Dr. says they can go back outside, they will be heading for freedom.... and hopefully warmer weather. Stay tuned.

March 30

Everything went smoothly. We were there at 8 AM. Will pick him up at 5:00. He has to stay inside for 7-10 days...... we will see how that goes.

March 31

All went very well for Zack, but had a scare with Jacky...... When I got home Monday evening Jacky's eye was swollen and seeping. Off to the vet where they found infection. SO, they sedated him, syringed goop from the eye socket, injected MEGA antibiotics and we came home. He is much better today. They both have to be inside for 7-10 days...... the weather should be much better by then. I will enjoy them, but worry that I won't want to let them go.

April 2

Everyone is back inside and feeling spunky.... do you think it is the Spring weather?

Zack did a flying leap over all obstacles on Tuesday to escape to his outdoor world. I didn't pursue him, lest he pop a stitch.... But yesterday morning he decided he would go where the food was.... inside. He seems happy. I am so glad the weather has turned warmer.... although thunderstorms are predicted for this afternoon. By the weekend it should be nice enough to let them go back outside.

Jacky's eye is doing well. The vet called this morning to check on him.... nice touch.

I do have to escape the house via the front door to get away, but that is a small price to pay.

Jacky loves to play and tease. Miffin is befuddled. Zack is patient. All is well.

April 5

They are romping today.... wrestling and chasing...... ready to go outside. Last night they were resting up. It Is a beautiful sunny day.... a great day to be outside.... can I let them go?

April 6.

Well, today was the day. They were ready, Miffin was ready, and strangely enough, I was ready. They left with tails held high and scampered off to rediscover old stomping grounds. I will be outside today, so will see how they are doing. Have to start spring schtuff before the rains set in. If I find them cold and wet they will be coming back inside. I think they have protective shelter in several spots.

It has been an interesting winter because of the twins. Now, I have to move forward and get ready for Spring and Summer and all that it will bring.

April 16

This morning Freddie came to breakfast. It was good to see him. Haven't seen Mom or Katie Kat in a long time. Hope they have found homes

May 8

Went out to plant some Marigolds around the patio this morning. Couldn't get the first one in the ground before Jacky showed up to help. He climbed up on my lap and needed petting and ear scratching before he was content to retire to the lily bed where he could supervise. The planting finally was finished. Now just the pots remain. Will get to them today.

May 9, 2015

The pots are done! All planting, front and back are done! Jacky helped!

This morning Jack, Zack and Freddie were all here for breakfast. Freddie is growing. He is about 9 months old, I think. Gentle disposition, just like the twins. They all have such intelligent eyes and loving souls.

May 18, 2015

Zack came to greet me from vacation limping on his hind leg. Uh Oh! Now what? But this morning he was better...... not limping. He is only a little over 1 year.... too young for arthritis.

Jacky is fine.... sweet as ever. And Freddie is still here. Hope to make friends with him this summer. :-)

June 10   Well, now it is Zack's turn. He had a raw spot on his hind leg.... the same leg he was limping on previously.... So, with much cunning and food, I was able to get him into the carrier and to the vet's. It turned out not to be serious.... just an open wound or sore for some cat-known reason. Shots of antibiotics and pain killers have taken care of it. Two days later, it looks MUCH better. And -- he lets me pick him up again...... I am not such a scary lady after all.

But, it is June and I am preparing to leave this beautiful, historic town.

It is time.

July 25

Well, yesterday was a trial.... today is turning out to be better. It was after 9:00 AM and no kitty faces looking for breakfast.... then 10:00...... 11:00...... about noon I saw Jacky in the garden napping next to Petey and Pup. I went out to see if he was hungry. He looked at me, but didn't move. My heart stopped...... something is very wrong...... He let me pick him up.... briefly, then moved to hide under the peony bush next to the deck. I took him some food and water, but he wasn't interested. He just stared into space.

I weeded a bit and watched him...... then, afraid that he would go under the deck and I wouldn't be able to reach him, I scooped him up and brought him into the house where I could watch him more closely

He went under the wing-back chair.... the skirt gives him privacy.... Miffin, of course had to snort and snarl and express his displeasure.

About 1:30, I saw Zack asleep in the garden…… went out to see if he was hungry…… or had they both gotten into something overnight? He did eat, but seemed preoccupied.

I called the vet, but it was too late in the day for them to be seen. The vet said to boil some chicken and try to get Jacky to eat something…. even the broth. We could be seen at 9:15 in the morning. Jacky wasn't interested in food, only sleeping.

I arranged a bed, a litter pan, and a food and water station near the back door, closed Jacky in the family room and went to bed…. wondering what I would find in the morning.

This morning, when I came downstairs, Jacky greeted me…. doing much better. He ate some of the chicken and all of the broth. I called and cancelled the vet appointment.

Then I looked out the window for Zack. I didn't see him, at first, but about 8:30 I saw him asleep under the peony bush…. an unusual place for him to spend the night. About 9:00, he seemed to be rallying, so I took his breakfast out…… Remember that sore on his hind leg a few months ago? Well, it was back…… I headed for the medicine cabinet. He let me put Neosporin on it (the vet said this was OK last time.) I don't think it lasted too long…. he was licking it when I looked out, later.

Tomorrow, I will be armed with bandages, Neosporin, etc. to see if I can fashion some sort of dressing that will stay in place and not let him lick it off……

WHAT NEXT? Jacky is eating again…. still sleeping a lot, I will keep him in another night and see how he is tomorrow…. He is so good inside, I am tempted to keep him in…… but then what? Zack and Freddie are still outside…… I can't bring them all in….

Don't know who is going to doctor them when I move......It makes me anxious. They are such sweet animals.

August...... The summer has been full of activity. The feral family is finally doing very well. The best news is that the folks who bought the house will love the twins. The family lives in another country. The parents purchased the house for their daughter who will be attending the local college and will be their residence when they can visit. The daughter was sad that she had to leave her pets behind and was delighted that she would have these beautiful, furry friends to care for.

At the end of August, we hugged each member of the feral family that we could catch and cuddle. Then, we bundled up Miffin.... No easy task, I may say... Made him as comfortable as we could in his carrier for the two day trip to Florida and my daughter and I started off to what was to be the next chapter on our lives.

CHAPTER

The Beginning

Cats have always been a part of my life... not always at the forefront, however. There were the Banty Chicks, for a 4-H project; the horses, that succeeded in keeping me actively occupied through the adolescent years; the dogs, that curled up on my lap in the evenings of early television. But there have always been cats... Even after I was married and had children to raise, there were cats... and dogs.

But then, in the middle years of my life, everything changed... and I mean everything. A divorce, the children went off to college, I went back to get a new degree, and the last, loving pet passed on.

Boldly, with the confidence that life would stabilize, I moved across country to begin a new existence. The only difficult part was that it didn't, nor could it, include a pet. There was no time or energy left in the day to give a pet the proper attention it deserved.

I moved back to my childhood home, then moved on to a new career, and finally found a cadence that allowed for more personal enjoyments and enrichments. And that meant that it was, once again, time for pets.

CHAPTER

Two Black Cats

It was a fairly normal Saturday morning—quiet with no obligations beyond enjoying a day at home.

The cats – Margaret and Squeak – had eaten and gone their separate ways. Margaret was about 8 now. She had come to me while I lived in New Hampshire. It was an unsettling time for me and I was comforted when she would appear for short visits.

Being small, I assumed she was still in her kitten years. She would let me pet her, but not hold her. We would sit on the back steps together until she had stayed long enough, in her mind, before wandering off across the back yards.

In our town, we had what were called "porch cats". As you drove down a street during the day, the front porches of houses would be hosting a gathering of cats…. Did they all live there? No one knew… they could just gather there to enjoy each other's company for the day. But also, litters were often birthed under those porches and would live together in their shelter. Margaret could have been a porch cat.

She didn't come every day, at first. Nor did I consider feeding her, at first. But, as the summer wore on, I pondered her eating opportunities – she didn't seem to be growing much – so, I purchased individually packaged, moist tidbit pouches—to keep on hand, just in case.

At first, she would only eat a few niblets on the back steps. In time, she would come all the way into the kitchen. And yes, by the time the arctic New Hampshire winter had set in, she was in the house, full time.

For an outside cat, she settled in quite well. On good days, she still enjoyed going outside, but she always came in by evening. Because she came to me when I was troubled --quietly, without agenda, and helped me sort out priorities - much the way my mother used to when I was young – I named her Margaret, after my mother. When the time came for me to move from New Hampshire to Ohio, Margaret moved with me.

Squeaker was a gift. His mother had been taken to the shelter to be put down. Having been dropped off, heavy with kittens, the shelter called my daughter-in-law, who was a foster pet caregiver, to take the cat until the kittens were born and then homes would be found for all. She happily accepted the task.

It was the mother's first time in childbirth. She was young, the litter was ample, and when the time came for the last kitten to be born, the mother was too spent to help. Amy pulled the helpless ball of fur into the world and hurried to stimulate its breathing. It took a few tense moments of rubbing and blowing, but soon the tiny life began to breathe on his own.

We often wondered if a lack of oxygen for these precious few seconds led to his inability to meow. He only squeaked.

When he was old enough, he was driven the five-hour distance from Amy's house to mine to become a companion to Margaret. Although he came with the name of George, he quickly became known as Squeaker.

Squeaker was a delight! Not as bright nor as quick as Margaret -- My daughter once made the remark, "You went to school on the short school bus, didn't you, Darlin'?" But, he was sweet, loving, and brought humor to the household.

Now, Margaret wasn't nearly as impressed, nor entirely hospitable. She had been the queen for many years and wasn't sure what to do with this sprightly upstart. She didn't like to play. Although she did have some small, soft, balls she chased around the house, she wasn't about to share them. She wasn't hostile, she just wasn't warm. I often wondered what went on while I was at work.

Today, however, I was home, relaxing in the family room which was adjacent and open to the kitchen. Three or four years had gone by since Squeaker had come to us. I couldn't describe the cats as buddies, but they had accepted each other as cohabitants.

Now, as you know, cats are curious... Margaret, especially.

In the kitchen, between the far wall and the dishwasher, was a bank of drawers in which I kept schtuff... you know... top drawer – silverware, second drawer – dish towels, etc. And, in the bottom drawer I stuffed extra plastic grocery bags – what else do you do with them?

As I enjoyed a rare moment reading a favorite book, Margaret wandered into the kitchen... Squeaker had not been seen for a while. She approached the bank of drawers and started to pull at the bottom drawer with her front paw... she had not been declawed.

I stopped reading to watch her. My curiosity being aroused, I watched as she systematically worked at that drawer until she got it open... open far enough so she could effortlessly hop in and comfortably move around. I wondered if she was just curious or if she planned to settle in for a nap. Had she done this before? Had she done this often? She seemed absorbed in her endeavor – rustling around in the plastic bags.

Now, as you know, cats are also devilish, mischievous.

Suddenly, I heard another sound.... Kathump, kathump, kathump... the sound of Squeaker bounding down the stairs. He raced through the family room and headed straight for the kitchen and the open drawer containing Margaret. Without missing a beat, he planted himself firmly on his haunches and, with his two front paws, pushed the drawer shut!

Then, with a decided look of satisfaction, he turned and headed back upstairs.

My first impulse was to leap up and rescue Margaret... but then, a second thought appeared. What if this had happened before? What if this should happen while I am at work?

Margaret was a bright cat. Maybe I should give her a moment and see what happens next. So, I stayed quiet on the couch and watched.

I heard movement in the drawer... and, amazed, I saw the drawer open a crack. More movement, more opening. More movement, more opening... until the opening was large enough for Margaret to reach out and push the drawer further open from the inside. Then, effortlessly, with the regal grace only cats have, she leaped out of the drawer, casually flipped her tail, turned her back on her would-be prison, and slowly sauntered away as if nothing had happened.

I was speechless.

Either this was a common occurrence or Margaret had quickly assessed that if she pushed on the back of the cabinet, it would force the drawer to the front and create an opening.

I won't go so far as to say the look on her face was smugness, nor even self-satisfaction, but I also was pleased not to see a look of vengeance.

Apparently, this was not an unusual activity on a normal week-day morning.

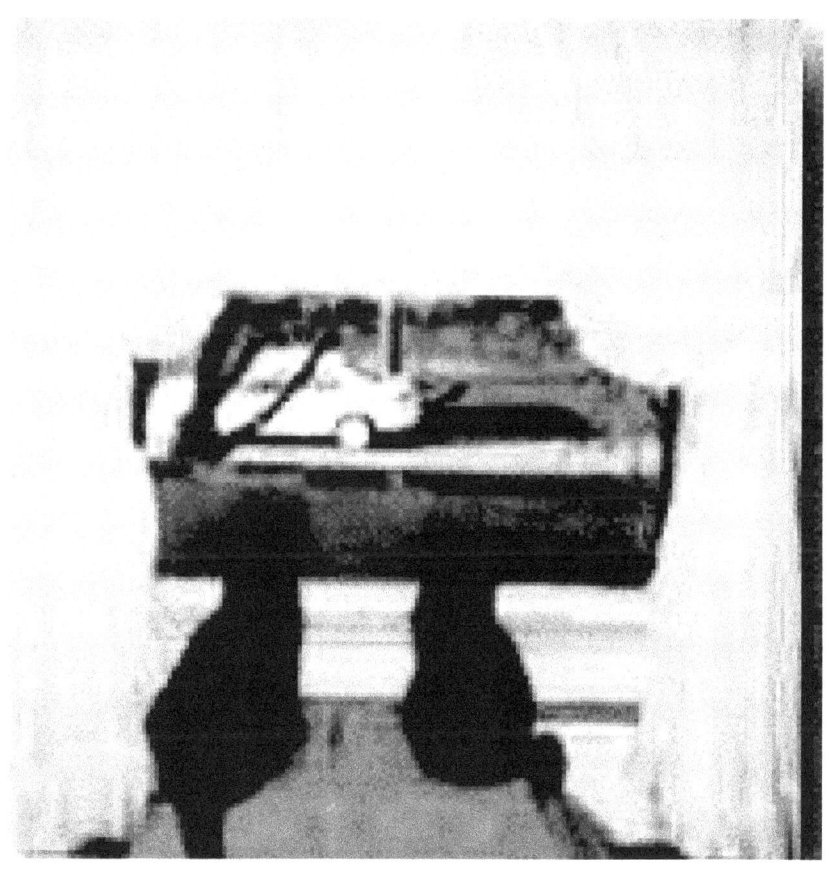

CHAPTER

Squeaker's Surprise

My workday was erratic. Being the Executive Director of an historic house museum meant that most days were long and many were longer. But, whatever my arrival time at home Margaret and Squeaker would always come running to meet me. I looked forward to this time.

Of course, for them it meant dinner, but for me it meant that someone was happy to see me.

One very usual evening had a very unusual greeting, however.

As I closed the door, and placed all the work-related totes to rest, Margaret came around the corner and sauntered over to say, "Welcome Home, and how was your day, and when is dinner?" We talked while I petted her and waited for Squeaker to appear. No sign of him. No sound of him. Hmmm. This was a big house. Was he napping so soundly in one of the upstairs bedrooms that he had not heard the back door? Or the car come up the drive?

I began to walk around the house, calling his name. No response. I was becoming concerned. Although, he was a healthy cat, he had had a marginal start in life, and I did not know if that meant anything medically as he grew older.

As I neared the stairway to the second floor, I could hear a very faint sound... a strange sound that I couldn't identify.... a sort of soft thumping, a sort of bell ringing, a sort of cadence amidst his plaintive meowings.

I called again, the sounds came closer. Then, as I approached the foot of the stairs, I could hear it more plainly... Thump, thump, jingle, meow. Thump, thump, jingle, meow. And now I could see him.... He was coming down the stairs with the most confused and painful look on his face.... Thump, thump, jingle, meow.

I was torn between feeling pain for him and laughing. Poor Squeaker had been playing with one of those plastic, lattice balls with the bell inside. Apparently, he stepped on it wrong and one of his toes had slipped inside the lattice. As he tried to remove it, the toe swelled to the point he couldn't get it off. The more he walked, the worse it got.

He was torn between answering my calls and feeling pain, but he tried to come greet me. It was coming down the stairs that hurt the worst.... Each time he stepped down, there was a thump, and then the bell would jingle, and he would meow with pain. Poor baby.

By now, I could scoop him up and take the weight off of the foot, but I could tell that the swelling had made the plastic tight enough that there still was pain. I tried to wiggle the ball off across the knuckles of his toes, but they were too swollen by then. This torture toy was not coming off.

It was good that I came from a family with tools. And it was good that everywhere I moved, I moved all those tools. I found a pair of wire cutters in the basement in my deceased father's toolbox. (All the while carrying and comforting Squeaker.) The tool was a bit cumbersome, and I was quite afraid that I might clip too much, but

I was successful in cutting the red plastic ball in enough places that I was able to extricate his swollen foot.

Immediately, his demeanor changed. The pain must have stopped with the release of the plastic pressure. I held him for a bit, but now that he wasn't encumbered by that evil red ball that had been biting his toe, he was eager to get on with supper. When I set him down, he ran up the basement stairs to tell Margaret about his harrowing experience with the red torture toy that pinched his foot and made strange noises.

I threw the ball away. Then, I tried to remember if there might be more than one hiding under a chair or sofa or behind a table leg waiting to attack my unsuspecting pet.

From then on, I only bought the soft, spongy balls that can be caught on a claw and gleefully tossed into the air only to bounce on the rug and harm no one.

They come in packages of three, in all colors, and are not aggressive. Even Matriarch Margaret has been seen playing with them.

CHAPTER

Miffin

In September of 2004 I was living in Marietta, Ohio.... A quintessential Midwest town. It had brick streets, Victorian houses, two colleges, Adena Indian mounds, hand-cranked river locks, and so much history. It was located at the mouth of the Muskingum River where it flowed into the Ohio River. And It was downriver from Pittsburgh.

In September of 2004 we were invaded by hurricane Ivan. Not only were the waters of both rivers rising because of the amount of rain, but upriver Pittsburgh had emptied its holding ponds in preparation for new, staggering amounts of rain from Ivan.

We had weathered hurricanes before, but everyone made extra attempts to stay safe from this one. Well, almost everyone. Somewhere, on the banks of the Muskingum, a family of a mother cat and her kittens had not been included.

Margaret was inside with me that stormy evening when there was a knock at the front door. Wondering who could be out in this storm, I answered it to find two friends standing on the porch...... "Oh, my gosh, come in." I said. "What are you doing out in this weather?"

We went into the front living room to be comfortable. Margaret disappeared back into the family room. The first friend said, "We know you recently lost your beloved Squeaker, so we brought you a new kitten to love." And the second friend reached into the zippered front of her jacket and pulled out the most bedraggled looking yellow kitten and held him up for me to see.

He had been pulled out of the waters of the Muskingum River at the end of Montgomery Street by a young couple on their way to shelter. They couldn't pass him by. He was the only one found. If there were more, they were lost, as was the mother. They put him in a pocket and headed for the Red Cross building for safety and assistance. They couldn't keep him. They had their own to care for. The Red Cross called my friend, knowing that she would find him a home.

She handed him toward me. He looked terrified.... and wet... and tiny.

Was there any decision to be made? Of course not. I took him from her. He fit in the palm of my hand.

We talked briefly about the circumstances and then they left.

I wrapped him in a towel to keep him warm. He was too tiny for Margaret's cat food, but I could give him some water with an eyedropper. I hoped he would make it until morning. Margaret was unimpressed.

In the morning, the rain had subsided enough that I could travel. I put him in Margaret's travel cage with warm towels and drove him to my veterinarian.

She looked him over, weighed him.... He weighed 18 ounces.... Gave me some flea soap.... He was infested with fleas which, if not eliminated, could actually kill him, there were so many.... and instructions on how to care for this tiny being.

My Fur Fix

I stopped at the local farm store to pick up formula and bottles and nipples and things that tiny kittens need to survive.

When I got home, I put him on the counter while I prepared his formula. There was a saucer there, so I put some in the saucer just to see where he was in his ability to take in food. He started to immediately lap up the formula. YAY! We weren't going to have to worry about tiny bottles and nipples and all that. He actually knew how to lap from the saucer. I poured in more formula. He lapped it all up. I felt better about his chances.

I bundled him up in another towel. I thought I would hold him for awhile and see how he did. I sat on the couch with him on my lap.... Margaret on the floor watching this whole scenario. What was I going to do with that intruder?

He slept. She went to make sure he hadn't eaten any of HER food. I relaxed.

When he awoke, a while later, I took him upstairs to the main bathroom to prepare his first flea bath. Warm water and flea soap with large, soft towels nearby. I filled the sink with lukewarm water and lowered him into it. He did well. He wasn't sure what it was all about, but he didn't struggle against it. I scrubbed with copious amounts of flea soap. The fleas fairly floated out of his fur. This stuff was good. It killed them on contact. I hoped it would not harm him.

He seemed to enjoy the warm water…. and perhaps the lack of fleas. Who knows how many had been biting him. After several minutes of scrubbing and combing, I lifted him out of the water onto the towel. The sink was black with fleas. We happily watched them go down the drain.

The bath routing was repeated several times before he seemed to be free of the monsters. Another trip to the vet reassured us that the fleas were gone and he was making headway. He had gained weight. His fur was soft and fluffy. He was responding to attention and he was sleeping quietly…. No more jerks and twitches.

Now that he was going to be a permanent member of the family, he should have a name. Hmmmm. Maybe Monty, since he was found at the end of Montgomery Street. But that seemed to be too adult for such a tiny soul. Maybe Mini Meow… Hmmm. Maybe "M" for Montgomery, "I" for IVAN… the hurricane… "F" for flood. Miffin. Yup, it seemed to fit him. So Miffin it was.

He grew steadily. We worked out the cat food and the eating stations. He learned about the litter box immediately. He would be an inside cat. Margaret still would go outside now and then, but she basically was an inside cat.

I did worry a bit about Margaret accepting this new intruder. She was not a warm and loving personality and I was concerned about her behavior while I was at work. But, when I came home in the evening all seemed to be well. Miffin was not the mischief maker that Squeaker had been. He was pretty much a solitary soul. I can't think of any noteworthy antics between them. They weren't real friends, nor were they great enemies. I will say, they coexisted.

For a few more years they coexisted. And then, one October day as I left for work, Margaret scooted out of the door with me. I remember saying, "See you tonight for supper." She always came back in the house at supper time.

I worked late that night and when I arrived home Margaret was not waiting at the back door. I never saw her again.

CHAPTER

Nala

Nala was an only cat. My grandson brought her home one day from a neighbor's new litter. It was to be his cat. However, being in high school, and living with his dad, Nala became their cat. And when my grandson graduated and went away from home, she became my son's cat.

My son had retired from the military and was studying for his Master's degree at a nearby college. Nala and he became best buds.

One day, he had to give Nala a bath. It was not something he had planned to do…. And be assured, it was not on her list of things to do either. It was a Wednesday, and on Wednesdays he didn't have school, so that was the day for doing errands as well as studying. He had left home early for a dentist appointment as well as errands and was gone all morning. By the time he returned it was close to one o'clock in the afternoon.

As soon as he opened the door, 12 week old Nala thundered toward him from across the house as if he had been gone forever. Her purr motor was running around six thousand RPM as she bounded around his feet, throwing herself at his shoes like they were invading chipmunks. Taking a couple of seconds to say "hi" he placed everything he was holding in his hands on the floor and scooped her up. Lifting her in one hand, he brought her up to his chest so he could pet her with the other. Being picked up, however, was not a part of her agenda and, like a fussy baby, she began pushing away from his shoulder with all four paws, purr engine still revving. With her hind legs braced against him, she rolled in his palm until she was lying on her back. Belly-up, she reached out with her front paws, grasping for the hand he was about to pet her with, and tried to pull it closer so she could nibble at his fingertips. Being a kitten, she still had the pin-like teeth all kittens have, and he put her down before she could use them.

Picking up all his packages, he walked to the breakfast table and put them down. That taken care of, he turned around and headed back the way he had come, toward the downstairs bathroom. Having been gone all morning, the call of nature was now close to screaming.

Still excited he was home, Nala had not been contented by their simple greeting, and was running through the house with all the energy only a kitten can have. Racing around the family room, turning the corners halfway up the wall as she went, she raced around pouncing on each of her stuffed toys as they appeared in her path. Slowing down just enough to rise up on her hind legs, she would hop forward, front paws and claws extended over her head as far as she could reach, and attack. Savagely descending upon her unsuspecting victim, she struck with tooth and claw. Biting into its plush stuffing, she racked and rended at its skin with her hind feet and claws. Once satisfied she had properly vanquished the villain, with her fur standing up on end, her tail bristled and pointing straight up in the air, and her back arched, she would prance and leap sideways away from the carcass, hopping to her next conquest.

Cower before her mighty ferociousness, puny toy, for she is savage in her viciousness, and thorough in her victory! She is kitty, fear her furry fury!

Leaving her to vanquish yet another victim, he rounded the corner and walked into the small, downstairs bathroom. Being the only person in the house, he saw no reason to close the door as he strolled over and lifted the seat and lid of the commode. While standing there, taking care of business, he looked over to see Nala climbing into her litter box, presumably to take care of her own business.

From the first day in the house, until he was sure she would use the litter box on her own, every time he went to the bathroom, he would take her with him and put her in her litter box so she would get the idea of its purpose. So, it wasn't strange to see her scraping at the litter while he urinated. He paid her no mind. No mind, that is, until she launched herself out of the litter box, over the side of the box, across the tiny bathroom, toward the side of the toilet bowl.

Being a kitten, I am pretty sure she had not read a single thing written by Isaac Newton, so she had no idea that a body in motion tended to stay in motion. Also, never having encountered porcelain while on a ballistic trajectory, she had no clue it gave no surface to little claws. The motion Newton spoke of carried her from the litter box to the rim of the toilet, and all the way to the bottom of the bowl. She may not have known these things beforehand, but as she went skidding over the edge, reaching back like she was lunging for the edge of a cliff as it slipped away, her eyes jumped wide open and she mouthed the kitty equivalent of "Oh Crap!" It didn't seem to help. The entire effect was not unlike a stick of dynamite being tossed in a rather small pond, except no dead fish floated to the top of the bowl.

Toilet water flew everywhere! Rivulets burst against the inside of the toilet, the seat, and the lid. What seemed to be bucketsful splashed halfway up the wall, cascaded across and down the side of the sink and wash basin, and, of course, splattered all over the front of my son's shirt and jeans.

And all he could do was stand there, stunned, immobilized, and watch. Not even realizing he was still busy.

Somehow, in the midst of all her thrashing, she was rewriting the laws of physics. Twice the amount of liquid the bowl could possibly hold splashed over every available surface. She was even able to make the splatter turn corners, and soak surfaces not so readily available. Time itself seemed to expand. Every thrash, every splash, hung suspended in front of his eyes, frozen in an infinite second before moving on to the next instance.

And all he could do was stand there, stunned, immobilized, and watch. Not even realizing he was still busy.

Even though it seemed to last an eternity, the whole thing was over in little more than a couple of seconds, and by some miracle she was able to find traction. Sopping wet, she exploded from the toilet.

Yes, 12 week old Nala had her first bath that day.

Her bed was on the floor in my Grandson's room but was soon abandoned for the more spacious and comfortable foot of the bed.

But, one of her favorite spots was on my son's shoulder while he worked and studied.

On the south wall of the great room were two sliding glass doors which led out onto the patio where local strays and other wildlife often rested. One frequent visitor was a pea hen. We named her Penelope. She didn't come when called, but she did respond to cereal. Nala found her fascinating.

Nala's life was pretty pleasant until one day she was invaded by myself and my cat, Miffin.

I had been retired for a few years and it was time to downsize. Since my son lived in Florida, it seemed only sensible that I live near him. So, while I searched for a new home for myself and Miffin, we lived in his house.

Now, Miffin had known other housemates. He knew Margaret, while he was growing up. And he knew the twins, Jack and Zack, until we moved south. He was not confrontational. Nala, on the other hand had been encroached upon. She was not used to sharing and wasn't sure how it was supposed to work. What was that awful odor in her litter box?

Food was not an issue, since Nala would only eat fish and Miffin did not care for fish. He only ate manly food like beef and chicken and such. So, each one had their own eating area and had no trouble respecting each other's dining space.

Napping space was another matter. Miffin preferred my lap (as often as possible). And Nala would curl up on the back of my son's overstuffed leather chair. However, when it came to napping space in front of the patio doors there was a problem. Although there were two large sliding doors, it seemed the sun only shone on one spot at a time. It was many moons before that space finally was peacefully shared.

Miffin would try to hide from Nala by disappearing behind the entertainment center which stood between the patio doors. However, it became a quest for Nala to seek him out and chase him from his refuge. She also thought he made a good sparring partner as she lay in wait for him to come out. Bat, bat, bat. Miffin often looked bewildered by her actions. Margaret had never done that. Nala often felt satisfied that she had gotten the best of this beast.

But Miffin was aging by this time. His intestinal system was breaking down and after about a year of trying to learn how to play with Nala, he left this earth. We all missed him.... Even Nala.

She would look for him in all his old hiding places, and even on my lap. Oh yes. My lap became a new destination for napping. And so, Nala became my son's cat with me as a backup.

When my son accepted a job out of the country and would be gone for 4 months at a time, Nala, for all intents and purposes, became my cat. Oh, when he would come home for a month's leave, she would make him feel loved. She even missed him when he was gone and would spend time sleeping on his unlaundered shirt, which he left on the floor of his closet. But, for the most part, she and I had our routine.

She would wake me in the morning with an insistent tone and would climb on my torso backwards and wave her fluffy tail across my face. "I'm hungry! It's time to get up and feed me!"

And so, each morning I would be sure to feed her first before I started my morning coffee.

By now we were in a different house. My son was tiring of the stairs in the townhouse and had a house built which was only 1 floor. The big patio doors were now replaced with French doors which led to a screened in lanai.

During the cooler winter months, the weather was lovely enough that we could open the French doors and Nala could leave the familiar indoors and venture out into what we humans call fresh air. On many a winter morning, Nala would wait for her breakfast out on the lanai. It was quite interesting out there.... There were birds and rabbits and such, but no pea hens and no stray cats or dogs or raccoons.... You know, familiar visitors.

When she had had enough of morning air, she would come in and eat her fishy breakfast. She loved all fishy food.... tuna, shrimp, whitefish, even one that claimed to be scallop flavored. Wet or dry was fine, as long as it tasted like fish.

Right around 2020, because of a pandemic called Covid 19 which led to shortages of manpower in all industries, there became a shortage of goods. Cat food was one of those shortages. I would drive from grocery store to grocery store looking for anything that said fish flavored cat food. When found, I would buy as much as I could. There were limits sometimes... after all, there were other cats who liked to eat, you know. But, I did the best I could. Every now and then I would arrive home empty handed to be greeted by such a look as any cat could produce.

What do you mean there is no cat food?

The new house was an open plan. The great room being in the center of the house with doors to other rooms at the sides. The lanai was one of those rooms. Off of the back of the great room, its entrance was glass French doors. The leather sofa was positioned perpendicular to the French doors.

In the evenings, while my son was out of the country, Nala would sit on the sofa next to me, or nap on my lap.

In Florida, during the peak of summer heat, we have storms…. Heavy downpours with booming claps of thunder and sky-lighting streaks of lightening. We have them often enough that most of the time we take them in stride.

However, one quiet, summer evening, as we were sitting on the sofa, watching TV, a sudden storm produced such a clap of thunder and a streak of lightening that sliced the sky with such a brilliance that it lit up the entire surroundings. This startled Nala. She sat straight up, faced the lanai and with eyes as round as saucers produced a look that said," What's lightening?"

In her 10th year, Nala became quite the cuddle cat. She would nag my son until he stopped working at his computer and followed her to his favorite chair. As soon as he sat down, she was in his lap. It was nap O'clock. They did this every day until it was time for him to leave again for four months. Then she would curl up on my lap for her evening nestle.

When she was about six, the vet had mentioned that we needed to keep an eye on her kidney's. I asked what that meant. What were we supposed to do? She had her regular checkups and the best of care. But, now, at 10 she was spending much more time sleeping.

My son had been gone about a month when I noticed that she was spending more time sleeping on his shirt on the floor of his closet instead of sleeping with me. She also was not eating her favorite food as much or as often. When she didn't come out for breakfast one day, but stayed all morning on his shirt, I felt something was not right. Even when I picked her up to put her in her carrier she did not protest.

I took her to the nearest animal hospital. After examination, the Dr. said it could be a number of things.... Had she ingested anything foreign? Was she using her litter box regularly? He would take more x rays, explore more possibilities and run more tests, and he would give me medication for her.

One of the medications was to be applied to her ear. She would wash the ear and lick her paw, ingesting the medication. The other was a liquid from a syringe. I remembered that she loved the taste of the hairball ointment, so I mixed the liquid with the ointment and she happily licked my finger until it was all gone.

I texted my son. I told him all that the Dr. had told me about her condition. He said that when I was comfortable with the situation, I should do what was best for her.

The next morning, she ate some food and seemed better. Later in the day the Dr. called with the new test results. It was renal cancer. That she was in great discomfort. I asked if, with medication, we could keep her comfortable until my son got home in about a month. The doctor said she only had about a week or 10 days at best.

Not wanting her to suffer for that long I decided to take her back that day. It was a heartbreaking decision.

My son has retired. He has a new cat. Yes, she is a rescue cat. Yes, she is black. Yes, they have a designated "kitty time." Yes, they are in love with each other.

Her name is Moya. She spends a great deal of time on the lanai napping in my wicker wingback. She waits by the garage door for my son to return from errands. He built a climbing tree especially for her. She loves it. The top level is above the lanai door. It's called "The Penthouse." She watches television from there in the evening. Perhaps in a year or three, there will be a chapter called "Moya."

ABOUT THE AUTHOR

Lynne Bodry Shuman was raised in New England. She recently lived in Marietta, Ohio, an historic town on the Ohio River. She now lives north of Tampa, FL.

During her creative years, Lynne has published A Guidebook for Northeast Indiana, was a co-author of The 50th Anniversary of Fort Wayne Youtheatre... a commemorative, and provided the photo research for Fort Wayne Citiscapes... A history of Fort Wayne, IN. She also wrote, directed, and narrated two award-winning educational videos for the historic house museum in Ohio which she most recently managed.

After 30 years as a Not-For-Profit administrator, Lynne is now retired. Although she loved her work, she thought, at 70 years of age, it was time to play. After years of writing as part of her work, she wanted to concentrate on gathering together some of the more interesting chapters of her life.

She has since written and published two books on travel: Travels With Time Share, Extraordinary Adventures by Ordinary People, and Glasgow to Heathrow – By B&B and Car.

This book has been teasing her for years. With all the personalities of these rescue cats, the book had to be written and shared. Enjoy!

www.ingramcontent.com/pod-product-compliance
Lightning Source LLC
LaVergne TN
LVHW061040070526
838201LV00073B/5126